Count Up From Six

By Amanda Gebhardt

 Class is out. It is time for snacks.

I found six snacks.

"Get ten, Sis," says Ken.
"Ten kids need snacks."

Ken sets a box of
snacks down.

 Ken will get ten drinks.

I must get ten snacks.

 I can count up from six.

I can count up from six to ten.

Six ...

seven, eight, nine, ten!

We all get a snack
and drink. Yum!

Now we can play!

math words

count	seven
eight	six
nine	ten

sight words

a	says
I	two
from	We
of	

diphthongs

/aw/al

all

/ow/ou, ow

count	now
down	out
found	

Try It!

Can you count up from six to ten?

Can you count up from four to ten?

Class is out. It is time for snacks.

I found six snacks.

"Get ten, Sis," says Ken. "Ten kids need snacks."

Ken sets a box of snacks down.

Ken will get ten drinks.

I must get ten snacks.

I can count up from six.

I can count up from six to ten.

Six ...

Seven, eight, nine, ten!

We all get a snack and drink. Yum!

Now we can play!

Published in the United States of America by Cherry Lake Publishing Group
Ann Arbor, Michigan
www.cherrylakepublishing.com

Cherry Blossom Press is an imprint of Cherry Lake Publishing Group.

Library of Congress Cataloging-in-Publication Data has been filed and is available at catalog.loc.gov.

Cherry Lake Publishing Group would like to acknowledge the work of the Partnership for 21st Century
Learning, a Network of Battelle for Kids. Please visit http://www.battelleforkids.org/networks/p21
for more information.

Printed in the United States of America
Corporate Graphics

Amanda Gebhardt is a curriculum writer and editor and a life-long learner. She lives in Ann Arbor,
Michigan, with her husband, two kids, and one playful pup named Cookie.